How Does My Garden Grow?

2nd and Pine: 2022

Photographs and text by Atwood Cutting

How Does My Garden Grow?

2nd and Pine: The 2022 Sequel

Photographs and text by Atwood Cutting

ISBN:
979-8-9865768-2-4
Copyright 2022
Echo Hill Arts LLC
Colorado Springs, CO

In April of 2020, we arrived with a cat,
a car full of plants, and my plan for a garden.

Both side yards would be for the birds.

Introducing our horseshoe pit and the Duke of Tulips.

Croquet,
Anyone?

In 2021, David turned the back patio into a summer dining/gameplaying/bedroom/garden center.

Then, he built me a cold frame.

Inside the house, prisms in the front window created rainbows sliding across the ceiling and walls.

2020

When we moved in, the view from the front window
left a lot to be desired.

So, we immediately planted two Redbud trees.
Next, we added Asters, Lilacs, Lambs Ear, roses,
a Saucer Magnolia and two Sweet Bays.

David patched the front walk, while I planted more Redbuds, some raspberries, and orange milkweed.

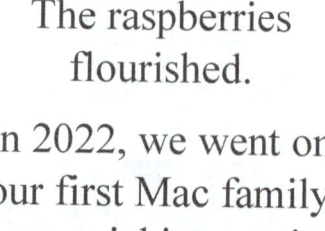

The raspberries flourished.

In 2022, we went on our first Mac family berry-picking sortie!

Each spring, those Redbuds delighted. As the greenery filled in along the front walk, I envisioned a sitting spot.

In 2022, David built a little conversation terrace there.

At last, a charming private garden separates us from 2nd street so that we can barely see the neighbors or the passing cars.

In another year, our tiny front yard should make us feel totally sequestered.

Now, on to the delights of the back yard.

Over the past three summers, I have painstakingly tended my struggling patch of Butterfly Weed in order to provide a nursery for the Monarchs.

Swallowtails, blues and yellows have come, too.

I shall call 2021 "the Summer of the Sunflowers."

You can pick your pathway to walk through the gardens.

Despite a heatwave in 2022, Hosta, Hibiscus, Iris, Lilies, Mimosa, Phlox, Poppies, Tulips and Zinnias keep shining.

What could be more exciting than sharing a summer evening with some singing Cicadas?